INVESTIGATE!

MYSTERIES OF SPACE

WHERE DO STARS COME FROM?

BY JENNIFER LOMBARDO

Enslow PUBLISHING

Please visit our website, www.enslow.com.
For a free color catalog of all our high-quality books, call toll free 1-800-398-2504 or fax 1-877-980-4454.

Cataloging-in-Publication Data
Names: Lombardo, Jennifer.
Title: Where do stars come from? / Jennifer Lombardo.
Description: New York : Enslow Publishing, 2024. | Series: Mysteries of space | Includes glossary and index.
Identifiers: ISBN 9781978535244 (pbk.) | ISBN 9781978535251 (library bound) | ISBN 9781978535268 (ebook)
Subjects: LCSH: Stars–Juvenile literature.
Classification: LCC QB801.7 L66 2024 | DDC 523.8–dc23

Portions of this work were originally authored by Greg Roza and published as *How Are Stars Born?* All new material this edition authored by Jennifer Lombardo.

Published in 2024 by
Enslow Publishing
2544 Clinton Street
Buffalo, NY 14224

Designer: Tanya Dellaccio Keeney
Editor: Jennifer Lombardo

Photo credits: Cover (logo) AAVAA/Shutterstock.com; series background Molibdenis/Shutterstock.com; cover NASA/ESA/Hubble Heritage (STScI/AURA)-ESA/Hubble Collaboration; p. 4 sbellott/Shutterstock.com; p. 5 Yelloo/Shutterstock.com; p. 7 (top) NASA/JPL-Caltech; p. 7 (bottom) icemanphotos/Shutterstock.com; pp. 8, 13, 15, 29 courtesy of NASA; p. 9 ESA/Hubble & NASA, G. Folatelli; p. 11 NASA, ESA, Hubble Heritage Team; p. 16 NASA images/Shutterstock.com; p. 18 NASA Ames/JPL-Caltech; p. 19 Samorodskiy Oleh/Shutterstock.com; p. 21 NASA/SDO; pp. 23, 25 Marusya Chaika/Shutterstock.com; p. 27 NASA, ESA, Elizabeth Wheatley (STScI).

Printed in the United States of America

CPSIA compliance information: Batch #CSENS24: For further information contact Enslow Publishing at 1-800-398-2504.

CONTENTS

Words in the glossary appear in **bold** type the first time they are used in the text.

WHAT IS A STAR?

When we look up at the night sky, we often see tiny points of light no brighter than fireflies. Some ancient peoples thought they were the spirits of people who had died. Others believed they were where the gods lived.

Today, thanks to **astronomy**, we know that stars are giant, burning balls of gas and dust. They look small and dim because they're billions of miles away. If they were much closer, some would look like our sun, which is also a star.

EXPLORE MORE!

STARS AREN'T LIVING THINGS. HOWEVER, THEY DO HAVE WHAT WE CALL A LIFE CYCLE. WHEN THEY COME INTO EXISTENCE, WE SAY THEY'RE "BORN." WHEN THEY BURN OUT, WE SAY THEY "DIE."

BECAUSE STARS LOOK SO DIM TO US, THEY'RE HARD TO SEE IF IT ISN'T VERY DARK. THAT'S WHY YOU CAN SEE MORE STARS OUTSIDE OF A CITY THAN IN IT.

SO MANY STARS!

The stars we can see are only a tiny part of all the stars in the **universe**. It's impossible for someone to count them all, so scientists estimate, or guess based on what they know. This is hard because there's a lot they don't know, such as how big the universe actually is.

Scientists estimate that there are more than 100 billion stars in our **galaxy** and more than 10 trillion galaxies in the universe. Multiplying those numbers gives us 1 septillion stars, or a 1 with 24 zeros after it—and this is lower than the real number!

EXPLORE MORE!

SOME PEOPLE BELIEVE ALL THE STARS IN THE SKY ARE ALREADY DEAD. THIS ISN'T TRUE, BUT IT IS TRUE THAT WE'RE SEEING THEM AS THEY LOOKED IN THE PAST! THEY'RE SO FAR AWAY THAT IT TAKES YEARS FOR THEIR LIGHT TO REACH EARTH.

THERE IS ABOUT THE SAME NUMBER OF STARS IN THE UNIVERSE AS SAND GRAINS ON ALL OF EARTH'S BEACHES. ALL THE STARS WE CAN SEE IN THE SKY ARE IN OUR GALAXY, WHICH IS CALLED THE MILKY WAY.

INSIDE A GALAXY

Galaxies are where new stars are born. There isn't enough matter outside a galaxy for stars to form. Inside every galaxy are huge pockets of gas and dust called nebulae. Nebulae are where stars form, although not every nebula will create stars.

Hydrogen—the most common element in the universe—is the gas that makes up most of a nebula. The dust in a nebula is made up of small amounts of other elements. Nebulae are generally very thin clouds that are spread out over many light-years.

FROM EARTH, THE MILKY WAY GALAXY APPEARS AS A THICK LINE OF STARS.

FROM THE OUTSIDE, THE MILKY WAY GALAXY LOOKS LIKE A SPIRAL, LIKE THE ONE SHOWN HERE.

EXPLORE MORE!

A LIGHT-YEAR IS A MEASURE OF DISTANCE, NOT TIME. IT'S THE DISTANCE LIGHT TRAVELS IN ONE EARTH YEAR. THIS WORKS OUT TO ABOUT 6 TRILLION MILES (9 TRILLION KM).

THE STARTING POINT

Over time, a nebula attracts more gas and dust and starts to clump up in places. As the clump grows larger, its **gravity** grows too. This gravity pulls even more matter into the clump.

When it's big enough, the clump begins to spin, or rotate. The rotation causes gas and dust to form a kind of disk. The disk rotates faster, drawing in more gas and dust. This action creates a hot, solid ball called a protostar. "Proto" means something that comes before something else.

EXPLORE MORE!

PROTOSTARS LOOK JUST LIKE STARS, BUT THEIR CENTER, OR CORE, ISN'T AS HOT. THEY'RE HARD TO SEE EVEN WITH A TELESCOPE BECAUSE THEY'RE OFTEN BLOCKED BY THE DUST THEY'RE ATTRACTING.

THIS PICTURE SHOWS A NEBULA THAT SCIENTISTS HAVE NAMED THE BUBBLE NEBULA.

HEATING UP

The gravity that pulls a protostar together **compresses** the hydrogen gas in the nebula. When a gas compresses, the **atoms** that make it up bump into each other more often. These bumps create heat and light.

At this point, the heat and light **energy** flowing out aren't strong enough to overpower the protostar's inward-pulling gravity. Gas and dust continue to pour into the protostar, making it bigger and denser, or more tightly packed. The hydrogen atoms get so close that they fuse, or join together.

EXPLORE MORE!

AS A PROTOSTAR GETS BIGGER, IT TRAPS HEAT INSIDE ITSELF. WHEN IT GETS HOT ENOUGH, HYDROGEN FUSION STARTS.

THIS PICTURE WAS TAKEN BY NASA'S JAMES WEBB TELESCOPE. IT SHOWS A PROTOSTAR STARTING TO FORM. THE DARK LINE IN THE MIDDLE OF THIS HOURGLASS IS THE DISK OF THE PROTOSTAR.

A TRUE STAR

When hydrogen atoms fuse, they become helium atoms. This process is called nuclear fusion, and it creates energy. At this point, the protostar is a true star, and its heat and light come from nuclear fusion instead of compression.

When a protostar turns into a star, it sends out two huge jets of energy that blast away much of the remaining gas and dust. Instead of pulling matter into itself, the star powers itself through nuclear fusion. It doesn't get any bigger until it enters another phase.

EXPLORE MORE!

IT TAKES MILLIONS OF YEARS FOR A PROTOSTAR TO BECOME A STAR. SOME PROTOSTARS NEVER HEAT UP ENOUGH TO START NUCLEAR FUSION. ASTRONOMERS CALL THESE "BROWN DWARFS." SOME PEOPLE ALSO CALL THEM "FAILED STARS."

IN THIS PICTURE, THE OLDEST STARS ARE IN THE MIDDLE OF THE NEBULA. YOUNGER STARS ARE FORMING ON THE EDGES OF THE CLOUD.

ATTRACTING OBJECTS

The energy a star gives off while it's forming moves the dust of the nebula around, forming smaller clumps. As these clumps attract more matter, they get bigger and start to spin, just like the protostar. In time, these clumps of matter become planets, moons, and **asteroids**.

When the protostar becomes a star and blasts away the dust and gas around it, these objects are too heavy to be blown away. The star's gravity pulls them into its orbit. This is called a planetary system.

EXPLORE MORE!

SCIENTISTS CALL OUR OWN PLANETARY SYSTEM THE SOLAR SYSTEM. THIS IS BECAUSE WE USE THE WORD "SOLAR" TO TALK ABOUT OUR OWN STAR. THE WORD "STELLAR" IS USED TO TALK ABOUT OTHER STARS.

THIS PICTURE SHOWS THE SIZES AND POSITIONS OF THE PLANETS IN THE KEPLER-62 PLANETARY SYSTEM COMPARED TO OUR INNER SOLAR SYSTEM.

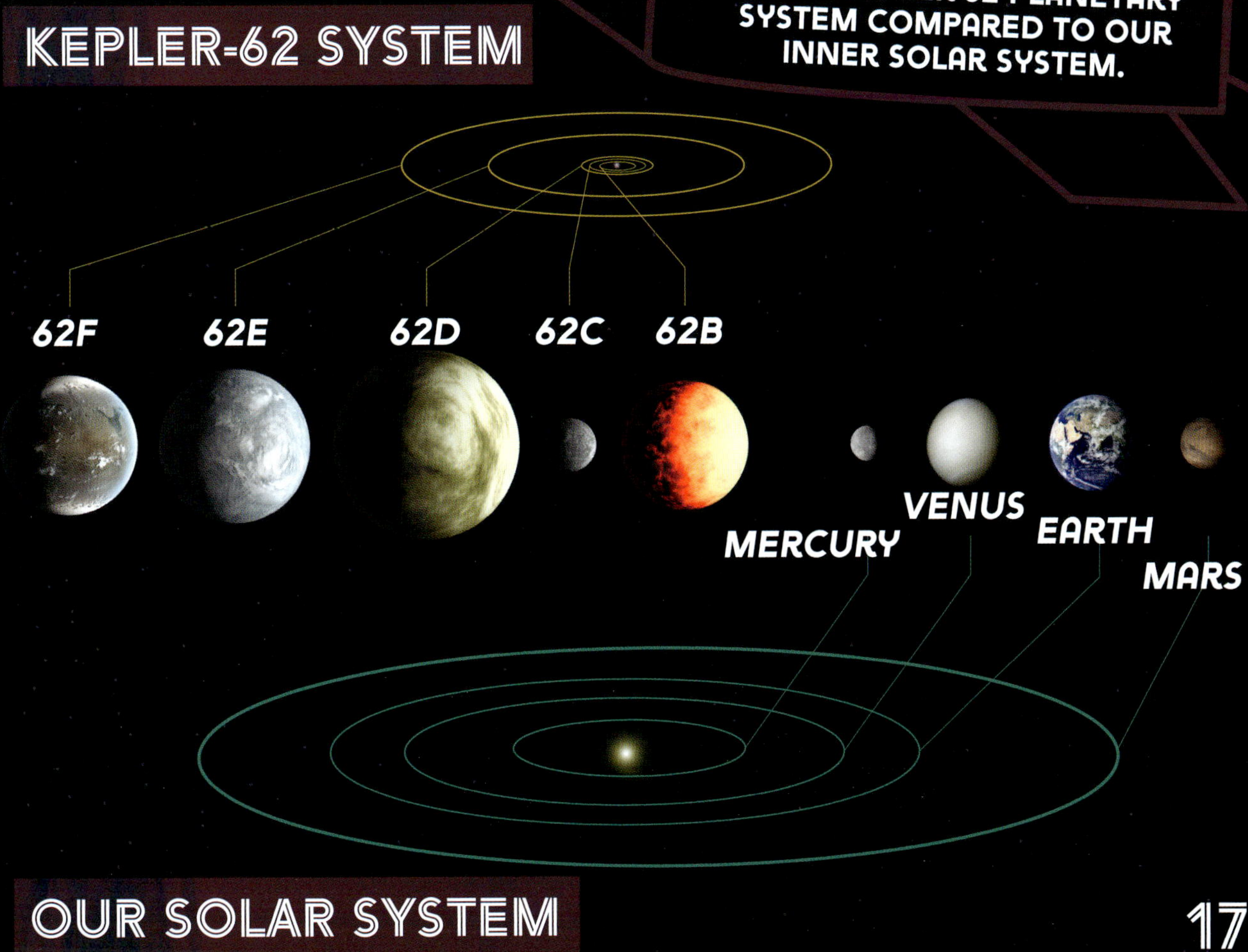

A LOOK AT OUR SUN

Not all stars are the same. Their life cycle depends on how they formed, how big they are, how hot they are, and how long they live. Let's take a look at our sun, the closest star to Earth, to better understand the lives of stars.

While a star is turning hydrogen into helium in its core, scientists say it's in a part of its life called the "main sequence." Our sun reached its main sequence between 4.5 and 5 billion years ago. It'll remain a main-sequence star for about another 5 billion years.

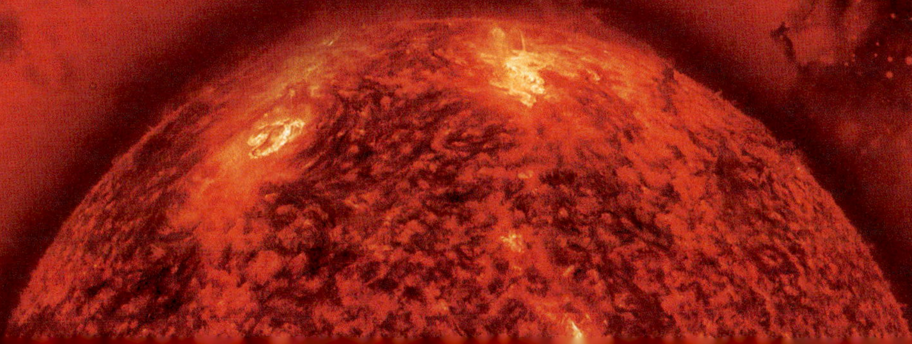

THE SUN GIVES OFF THE EXACT AMOUNT OF LIGHT AND HEAT NEEDED BY ALL LIVING THINGS ON EARTH. IF IT WERE BIGGER, SMALLER, OR IN A DIFFERENT PART OF ITS LIFE CYCLE, WE LIKELY WOULDN'T BE HERE!

EXPLORE MORE!

MAIN-SEQUENCE STARS ARE ONES THAT TURN HYDROGEN INTO HELIUM THROUGH NUCLEAR FUSION. ABOUT 90 PERCENT OF ALL THE STARS IN THE UNIVERSE ARE MAIN-SEQUENCE STARS.

THE NEXT STEPS

When the sun runs out of hydrogen, its core will shrink. The smaller core will have more gravity because it's denser. Increased gravity will cause helium in the core to fuse into carbon and oxygen.

At this point, the sun will turn from what it is right now—a yellow dwarf star—into a type of star called a red giant. The carbon **fuel** will make the sun even hotter and bigger. In fact, the sun will expand, or grow, so large that it will swallow Mercury, Venus, and maybe Earth as well.

EXPLORE MORE!

EVEN IF THE SUN DOESN'T SWALLOW EARTH, IT WILL BE SO BIG AND HOT AS A RED GIANT THAT NOTHING WILL BE ABLE TO LIVE ON THE PLANET. LUCKILY, THAT WON'T HAPPEN FOR BILLIONS OF YEARS!

THIS PHOTO OF THE SUN WAS TAKEN BY NASA. IT SHOWS A **SOLAR PROMINENCE** MANY TIMES THE SIZE OF OUR PLANET. EARTH'S SIZE IS SHOWN FOR COMPARISON.

Without the outward force of nuclear fusion, our sun's gravity will cause its core to cave in, or collapse. It'll become a hot, dense ball of carbon and oxygen about the size of Earth. The star will push out some of its matter to form a planetary nebula.

What's left—the slowly cooling core—will be a white dwarf. Billions of years after that, the white dwarf may turn into a black dwarf. However, scientists say the universe has existed for less time than it would take for a star to become a black dwarf, so none exist right now.

THIS PICTURE SHOWS THE LIFE CYCLE OF A YELLOW DWARF STAR LIKE OUR SUN.

LIFE CYCLE OF A SUN

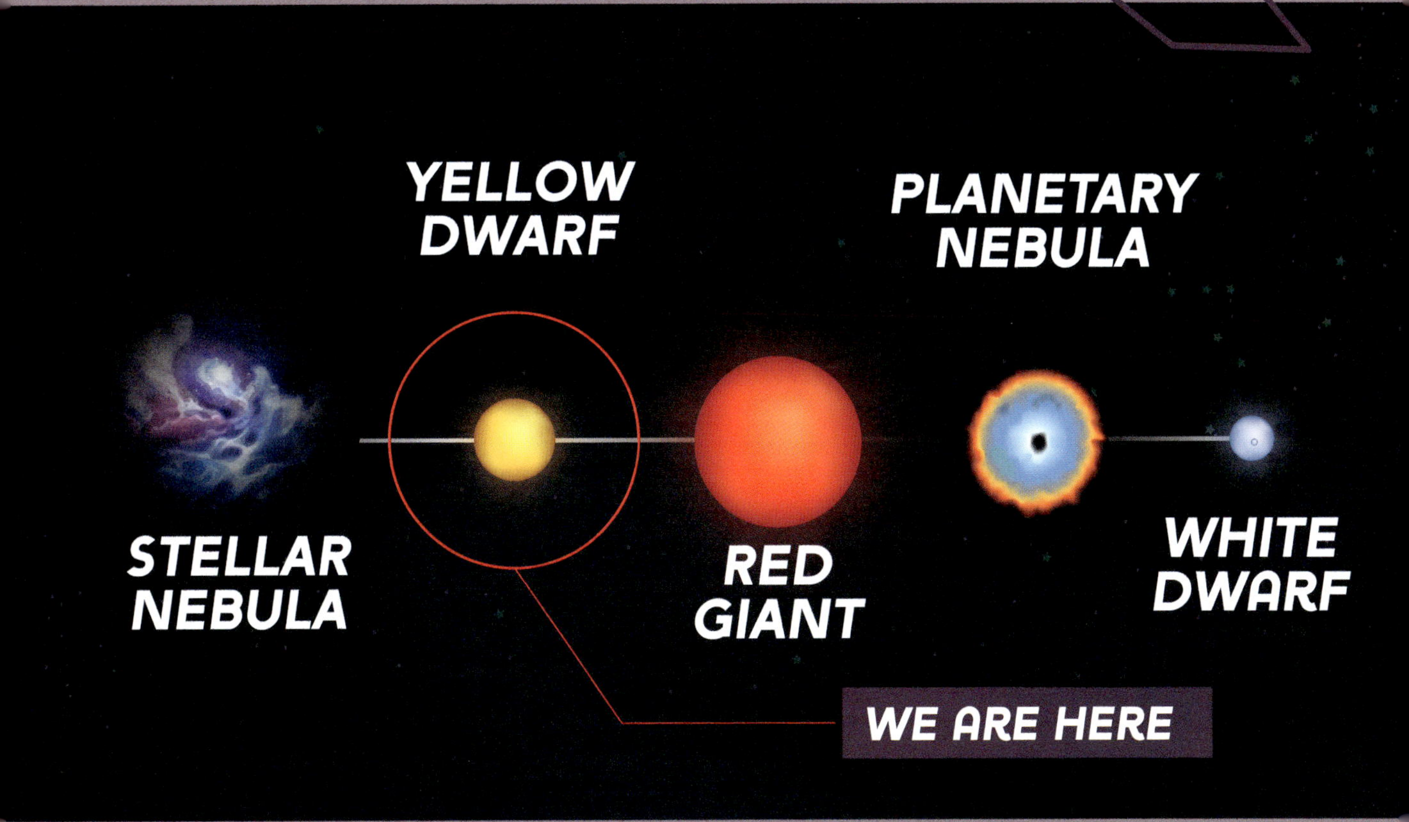

EXPLORE MORE!

PLANETARY NEBULAE DON'T HAVE ANYTHING TO DO WITH PLANETS. THEY GOT THIS NAME BECAUSE MANY OF THEM ARE ROUND, SO EARLY ASTRONOMERS USING LOW-POWER TELESCOPES THOUGHT THEY WERE FAR AWAY PLANETS.

OTHER KINDS OF STARS

Not all stars start out as yellow dwarfs. Red dwarf stars are much smaller. They have less mass and gravity. Red dwarfs burn hydrogen slowly compared to larger stars, and they last longer.

Another kind of star is a blue supergiant. These stars are some of the hottest and most massive objects in the universe. However, that doesn't mean they're the biggest! Mass is a measure of how much "stuff" something has in it. Imagine one flat sheet of aluminum foil compared to three sheets crumpled into a ball. The single sheet looks larger, but the ball is more massive.

THIS PICTURE SHOWS SOME OF THE DIFFERENT KINDS OF STARS AND WHERE THEY FALL IN A STAR'S LIFE CYCLE.

LIFE CYCLE OF A STAR

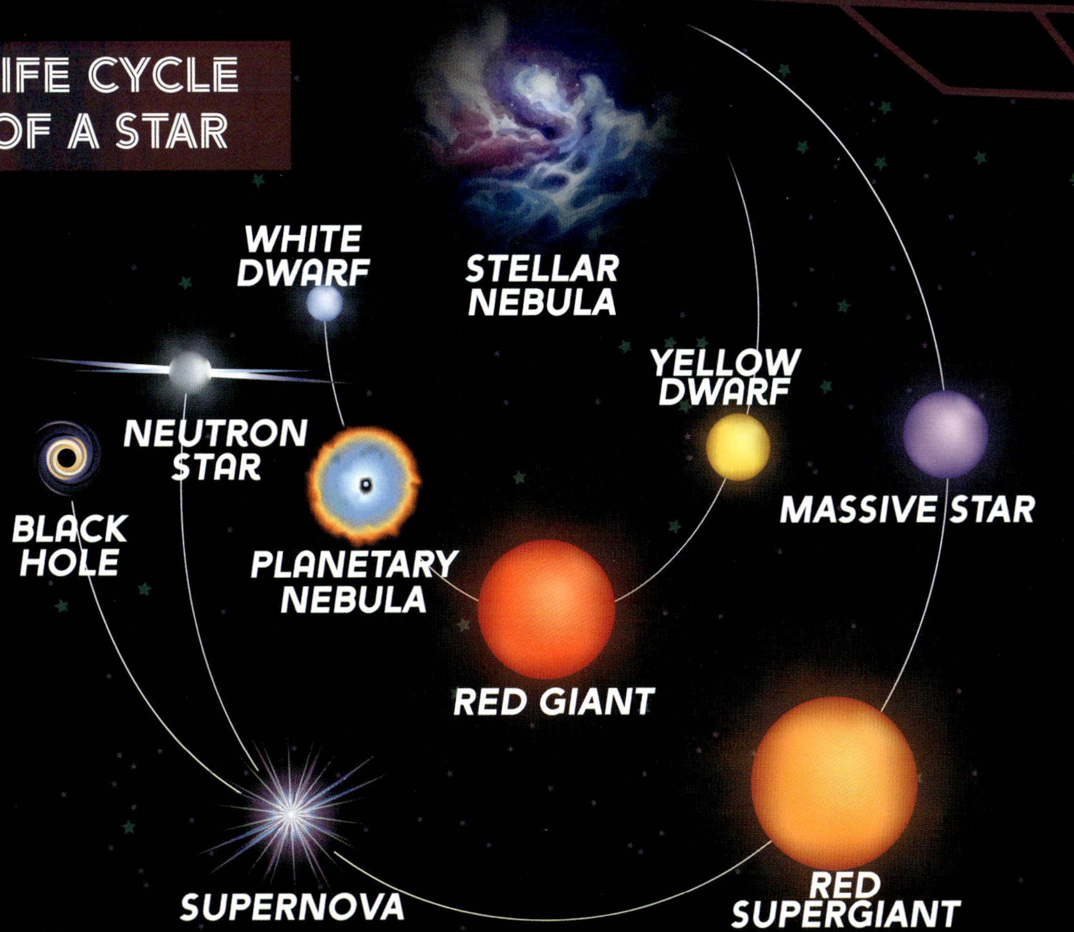

EXPLORE MORE!

MAIN-SEQUENCE RED DWARF STARS ARE THE MOST COMMON KIND OF STAR IN THE UNIVERSE. THE LEAST COMMON ARE BLUE STARS, ESPECIALLY BLUE SUPERGIANTS.

RED SUPERGIANTS

Some stars are so large that they burn through their hydrogen within a few million years. Since they started out large, they get even bigger when they exit the main sequence. They're known as red supergiants, and they're the biggest stars in the universe.

Like smaller stars, red supergiants collapse once they can no longer keep nuclear fusion going. However, because of their size, their life ends a little differently than that of smaller stars. There are two things that can happen after a red supergiant collapses: It can become either a neutron star or a black hole.

EXPLORE MORE!

SCIENTISTS HAVE SOME IDEAS ABOUT WHAT DETERMINES THE SIZE OF A STAR WHEN IT'S BORN, BUT THEY DON'T KNOW THE ANSWER FOR SURE. THEY'RE STILL WORKING TO FIGURE IT OUT!

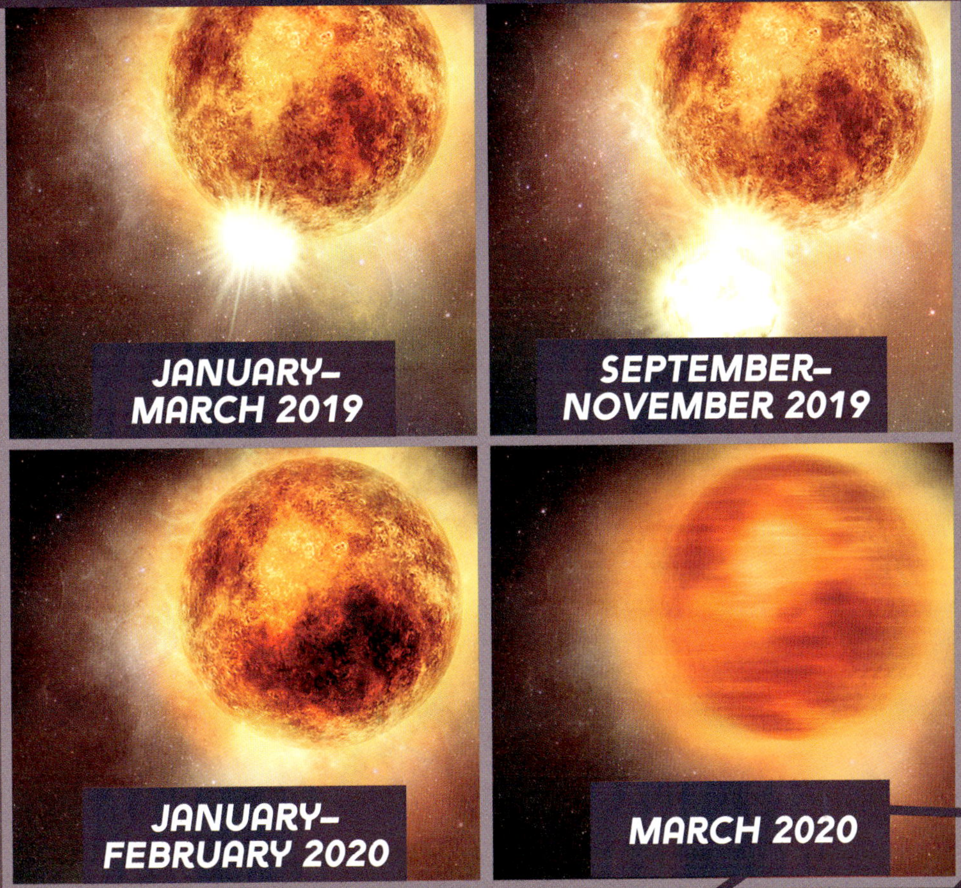

JANUARY–MARCH 2019

SEPTEMBER–NOVEMBER 2019

JANUARY–FEBRUARY 2020

MARCH 2020

THESE PHOTOS SHOW A RED SUPERGIANT CALLED BETELGEUSE LOSING A LARGE PART OF ITS MASS. THIS WAS THE FIRST TIME SCIENTISTS HAD EVER SEEN SOMETHING LIKE THIS HAPPEN.

TWO PATHS

When a supergiant collapses, it makes the largest explosion in the universe, which is called a supernova. This blows off the star's outer layers. A huge nebula glows for hundreds of thousands of years. The core can take one of two paths, depending on its size.

A star more than eight times larger than our sun may collapse into a tiny, superdense neutron star. At more than 20 times larger than our sun, so much matter is pulled into the core that the star becomes dense enough to create a black hole. This is an object with so much gravity that not even light can escape it!

EXPLORE MORE!

THE NEBULA CREATED BY A SUPERNOVA MAY COME TOGETHER TO FORM NEW STARS AND PLANETS. THEN THE PROCESS STARTS ALL OVER AGAIN!

IN THE YEAR 1054, PEOPLE ALL OVER THE WORLD SAW A SUPERNOVA FROM A STAR 6,500 LIGHT-YEARS AWAY. TODAY, WE CAN SEE ITS REMAINS IN THE CRAB NEBULA (SHOWN HERE).

GLOSSARY

asteroid: A small, rocky object circling a star.

astronomy: The science of the heavenly bodies and of their sizes, motions, and composition.

atom: One of the smallest bits of matter.

compress: To reduce the size, amount, or volume of something by pressure.

energy: Power used to do work.

fuel: Something used to make energy, heat, or power.

galaxy: A large group of stars, planets, gas, and dust that form a unit within the universe.

gravity: The force that pulls objects toward the center of a planet or star.

solar prominence: A large, bright feature that reaches out from the sun's surface, but stays anchored to its surface.

telescope: A tool that makes faraway objects look bigger and closer.

universe: Everything that exists.

FOR MORE INFORMATION

BOOKS

Armentrout, David, and Patricia Armentrout. *Stars.* New York, NY: Crabtree Publishing, 2022.

Patel, Parshati. *My Book of Stars and Planets.* New York, NY: DK Publishing, 2021.

Ringstad, Arnold. *Stars.* Mankato, MN: Child's World, 2021.

WEBSITES

BrainPOP: Life Cycle of Stars
www.brainpop.com/science/space/lifecycleofstars
Watch a movie, play games, and take quizzes to test your knowledge of stars.

Ducksters: Stars
www.ducksters.com/science/star.php
Read more cool facts about the life cycle of stars.

NASA Space Place: Stars
spaceplace.nasa.gov/search/stars
Learn more about stars with fun activities.

INDEX